This Notebook Belongs To:

DOODLES

Made in the USA
Las Vegas, NV
03 December 2023

82010262R00069